BEAUTIFULLY UNIQUE

RENAE SEWALL

Illustration by ANITA HATCHETT

BEAUTIFULLY UNIQUE

By Renae Sewall
Illustration by Anita Hatchett

This story is dedicated to my three Beautifully Unique daughters.
Words will never be able to express the love I have for you.
You inspire me each and every day with the love you
have for each other, your passion for life, and your courage to face
life's challenges. May you never lose that fire within!

With all the love in my heart,
Mom

My name is Sophia; I love to have fun and to make people smile.

But what I love most of all in the whole world is my family. I have a daddy and a mommy that love me as big as the world.

I also have two crazy, silly, and best-you-could-ever-ask for sisters that just happen to love me to pieces; even when I decide that what's theirs is mine when I need something to play with.

My family is very unique, which is something I didn't always understand and since I am all of six years old, I don't really care for things I don't understand. You see, my daddy has a really handsome shade of dark skin and my mommy and sisters have a lovely lighter shade of skin.

Then there is me, I am a fabulous shade of light brown. One day I started to get curious. Why are we so different? Lucky for me I have a Mommy that just LOVES answering the hundreds of questions I ask every day.

Mommy chuckled, kissed me on my forehead and said, "Well, my precious little girl, everyone is a little different and unique. You just happen to be the most perfect combination of your Daddy and me."

"But I feel different!" I said. "Daddy is darker than me and you are lighter, and I don't like my hair, it is too curly and fluffy. I wish It was smooth like yours."

Mommy smiled and stroked the side of my face; I think she could tell I was feeling a little out of place. "Sophia, my sweet little girl, don't you ever be afraid of being different. What makes us different is the very thing that makes each and everyone of us special and it just so happens that I am MADLY in love with your curls and all of your fluff and stuff."

That made me smile but I still wasn't sure what she meant. I didn't feel special, I felt different. Mommy thought for a moment "How can I explain it to you so that you may understand? Ahhhh! I think I know just the thing."

My eyes got bigger. "What?" I asked.
"It's a surprise." Mommy said, "Go put on your shoes so we can be on our way."

"Where are we going?" I asked.
"Nope, not a chance. It is a
surprise." She grinned.
So we got in the car and were
on our way...
destination unknown!

As we pulled up I noticed it was the Butterfly Garden. Yippee! I just love butterflies; they are just so pretty.

When we walked in I could not believe my eyes. There were more butterflies than I could even count. There were green ones with white dots and black trim, some with stripes like a tiger and even ones that blended right into the trees. There were hundreds of them all flying around together.

Mommy took me over to a bench so we could
sit down and get a closer look.
One landed on Mommy's head and it made us both giggle.

Mommy pointed and said, "Check out that one over there. What colors does that butterfly have?"
I looked at it really close, "Oh, that one is pretty, it has bright green, black, with a little bit of brown.

Mommy got all excited again and pointed out another one that was bright yellow, blue, green, black, and red!

"Do you know where all of the different butterflies come from?"
Mommy asked.
"No, I am only six years old silly mommy."
"Well my little smarty pants," Mommy laughed,
"They come from all over the world and that is why they all look so
unique with different colors."
"Wow, that is a lot of places!" I said.

"Now, my big hearted little girl, when you look at all of these butterflies are there any that aren't pretty?"
I looked around at the different colors and patterns as they were all flying together, it was the most beautiful thing my eyes had ever seen.
"They are all so pretty!"

With the biggest smile on her face Mommy said,
"That's right, my love, people are a lot like the butterflies
you see here today.
We all come from different places in the world, and we all come
in many shapes, sizes, and colors, just like our family. Don't you
think each butterfly's unique colors and patterns are what make it
special and beautiful?"

"Oh yes." I smiled.
Then Mommy said, "Each one of us has our own unique colors and patterns that make us unique. I want you to always remember how beautiful it is to be who you are."

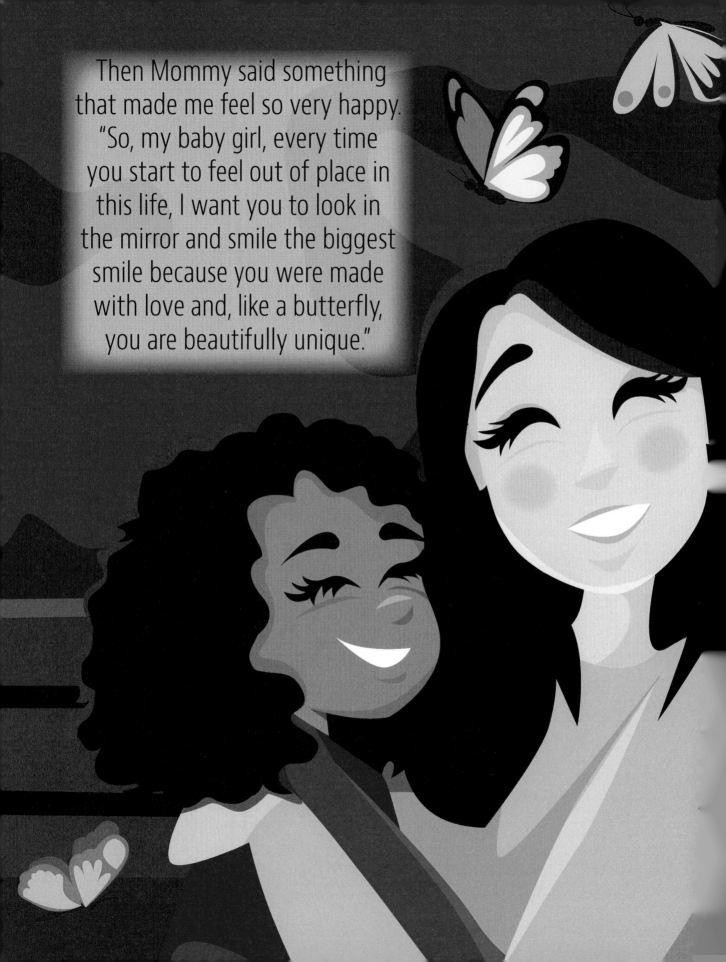

Then Mommy said something that made me feel so very happy. "So, my baby girl, every time you start to feel out of place in this life, I want you to look in the mirror and smile the biggest smile because you were made with love and, like a butterfly, you are beautifully unique."

So that is exactly what I did.
I smiled and said to myself...

I am Sophia, I am
beautifully unique!

My name is Sophia and I am here to tell you a story!
The story is about feeling different.
My family is unique, I am not like my Mommy, Daddy, or sisters,
which made me confused.
One day I asked my mommy why I was different,
so she took me on a little adventure to an amazing butterfly garden.
There, we saw so many different butterflies from all over the world while she
helped me understand that everyone is unique in their own way.